## It's Your Health!

# Puberty

ADAM HIBBERT

A⁺
**Smart Apple Media**

First published in 2004 by Franklin Watts
96 Leonard Street, London EC2A 4XD

Franklin Watts Australia
45–51 Huntley Street, Alexandria NSW 2015

Series editor: Sarah Peutrill, Editor: Sarah Ridley, Designed by: Pewter Design Associates, Series design: Peter Scoulding, Illustration: Roger Gorringe, Picture researcher: Sophie Hartley, Series consultant: Wendy Anthony, Health Education Unit, Education Service, Birmingham City Council

Picture credits: © Paul Baldesare/Photofusion: 17b, 31.© Dave Bartruff/Corbis: 12. Photo from www.JohnBirdsall.co.uk: 8, 14, 33 b, 40. Robert Brook/Photofusion: 4, 10, 45. BSIP, Barrelle/Science Photo Library: 23 t. © Mark Campbell/Photofusion: 23 b. © Jacky Chapman/Photofusion: 17 t. © Reg Charity/Corbis: 11. Chris Fairclough/Franklin Watts: 16, 18, 19b, 22, 36, 41 t. Franklin Watts: 15 b. © Stan Gamester/Photofusion: 39. © Charles Gupton/Corbis: 35 b. Dennis Hallinan/Alamy: 25b. © Walter Hodges/Corbis: 34. © Richard Hutchings/Corbis: 20. © Ute Klaphake/Photofusion: 21. Damien Lovegrove/Science Photo Library: 29. © LWA-Dann Tardif/Corbis: 41 b. © LWA-Stephen Welstead/Corbis: 33 t. © Cheryl Maeder/Corbis: 30. Dr. P. Marazzi/Science Photo Library: 19 t. © Brian Mitchell/Photofusion: 25 t, 37 t. © Roy Morsch/Corbis: 24. © Gabe Palmer/Corbis: 37 b. John Powell Photographer/Alamy: 26, 35 t. © Ulrike Preuss/Photofusion: 27. © Bob Rowan; Progressive Image/Corbis: 13 b. © Royalty-Free/Corbis: 9. © Paula Solloway/Photofusion: 38. © Christa Stadtler/Photofusion: 28. © Haruyoshi Yamaguchi/Corbis: 13 t.

Published in the United States by Smart Apple Media
2140 Howard Drive West, North Mankato, Minnesota 56003

Library of Congress Cataloging-in-Publication Data

Hibbert, Adam, 1968-
Puberty / by Adam Hibbert.
p. cm. — (It's your health)
Includes index.
ISBN 1-58340-592-5
1. Puberty—Juvenile literature. 1. Title. 11. Series.

QP84.4.H53 2005
612.6'61—dc22                 2004057857

9 8 7 6 5 4 3 2 1

# Contents

# Changes

As we change from children to young adults, we don't just grow taller. Our bodies change in many different ways. Some parts of our bodies will grow faster than other parts, and boys will grow in different ways than girls. We are often eager for these changes to arrive so we can feel more grown up. But sometimes, changes surprise or embarrass us. This book will look at both sides of the experience.

Despite just a few years' age difference, teenagers and younger children have very different needs and roles.

## Sexual maturity

The most important changes to understand have to do with our sexual maturity—becoming capable of having children. Until puberty, boys and girls cannot become parents. Our sexual organs do not produce the sex cells—the sperm or the egg (ovum)—that are needed for reproduction. At puberty, the hormones in the body change to begin the process of producing sex cells and to prepare the rest of the body for reproduction.

Puberty can be a bumpy ride—there will always be some thrills and some spills!

## Emotional growth

While our bodies are changing, our feelings and experiences are also changing. The strains on our bodies caused by puberty and growing can make us tired, grumpy, or confused about how we feel. But we can also have a great time experiencing new things about ourselves, our friends, and the possibilities that are opening up to us as young adults. It can be a roller coaster ride!

### It's your decision

We may think we know everything about puberty from an older brother or sister or from talking about it with our family or friends or in school. Some of us do, but many of us reach sexual maturity with some mistaken ideas about what it means. Will you investigate what you think you know or take your chances?

### It's your opinion

Around our early teens, most of us begin to desire more independence from our parents. It can sometimes feel like we are in a kind of prison. Before we know it, we will be out in the world, without the day-to-day support and care we once had from our parents. Should we enjoy it while it lasts, or is it normal to struggle against being treated like children?

### It's your health

This book looks at both the physical and the emotional sides of puberty. It tells only the general story, so do not be surprised or worried if the story does not exactly "fit" you—each of our experiences is unique.

# Growing

One of the first signs of the onset of puberty is a noticeable burst of growth in our arms, legs, and overall body length. This growth spurt usually happens around the age of 11 for girls and between 12 and 13 for boys. This is not the best time to be buying clothes you really love—they're only going to last you for a few months before you outgrow them.

## It's your decision

Can you eat healthily?
During a growth spurt, you might feel hungry a lot of the time. Instead of always reaching for chips and chocolate bars, grab a banana, an apple, or a sandwich. While you are growing, you can usually get away with fatty snacks without gaining weight, but once you reach adulthood, you'll pile on the pounds if you have poor eating habits.

## Growing pains

During a growth spurt, some people experience weird pains.

Bones grow at each end—for example, the thigh bone adds material where it meets the knee joint and where it meets the hip joint. Growing pains are usually a sign that your nerves are having to grow to "keep up." Rubbing painful areas, or having a massage, is the best way to ease these pains. If a pain like this lasts longer than a week, it may be due to something else—ask your doctor.

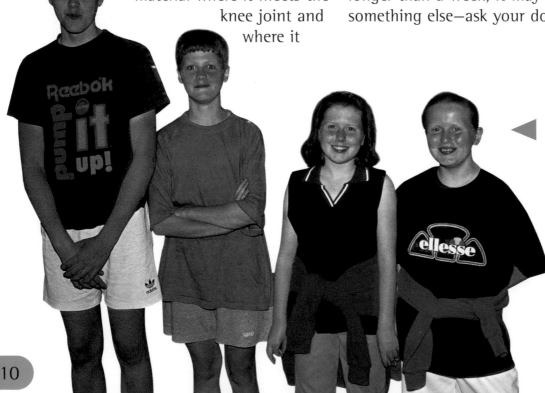

Some of us gain several inches in a single growth spurt—time for new clothes!

As the body adapts to new hormones and rapid growth, it burns more energy. It's quite normal to feel sleepy, especially in the early afternoon.

## It's your experience

"I can't understand it. I'm going to bed at a decent time but I feel so tired during my first class that my teacher keeps yelling at me for yawning."

Emiko, age 14

## Feeling Tired

Growing is also hard work for the cells in our bodies. They quickly use up the fuel we create from food. It is normal for our bodies to demand that we rest more often, and many of us find that we need more sleep than we did as children. Growing while we sleep also means that we might sometimes wake up in the morning feeling short of fuel—a sweet drink such as fruit juice can help.

## Shape shift

Our limbs do not necessarily grow at the same rate as each other. Some parts might grow more quickly than others. We might look a bit strange for a few months if our arms grow faster than our legs. But it all balances out in the end. Even the bones in our face, such as our nose bones, grow and change. We can see our adult face beginning to appear.

Girls grow before boys, but they don't grow as much as boys do.

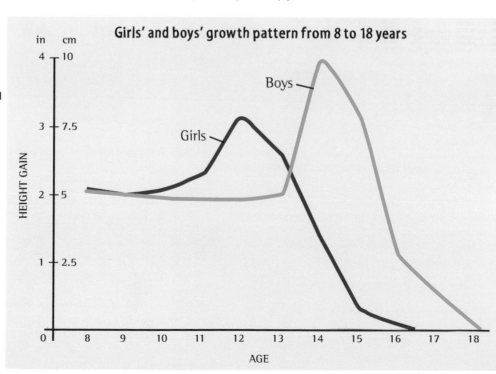

**Girls' and boys' growth pattern from 8 to 18 years**

Boys

Girls

HEIGHT GAIN

AGE

# Sexual maturity

Puberty describes the stage of our lives when our bodies change to become capable of reproduction. The timing of this stage varies from person to person. We continue to change and grow after puberty, but from that point onward, almost all of us are fertile, or biologically able to make a baby.

Burmese children wear festive costumes and sit at a banquet table during a coming-of-age ceremony in Pagan, Myanmar.

## It's your opinion

We all continue to learn about the world and each other throughout our lives. But at some point, society has to accept that we have enough experience to be treated as adults. How do you think that line between childhood and adulthood should be drawn? By age? By sexual maturity? By another measure?

## Social maturity

This change, from being a child to being a person capable of creating a baby, is a big step toward adulthood. In some societies, it is marked by a special event or celebration. In all societies, parents and other people around you will begin to recognize you as a young man or a young woman. However, it does not mark the end of childhood, which is defined by the law in most countries as being between 16 and 18 years old.

Two Japanese teens celebrate their coming-of-age ceremony, wearing traditional kimonos. Like an American high school prom, this event marks a step toward adulthood.

## It's your experience

"I hated being later to develop than my younger sister. She got taller than me when I was 12 and she was 11. I know it all works out in the end, but it made me worried at the time."

Hakaru, age 16

## Sooner or later

There is no "right" time for puberty to begin. No one likes to be left behind when all of their friends are having an experience, but it can be just as hard to be first as to be last. At least being last lets us see how others deal with the changes. For most of us, puberty will begin between the ages of 12 and 15, although it has happened to people as young as 7 or as old as 17.

Boys' height differences can be extreme but usually even out by their late teens.

## Biological maturity

Sexual maturity not only changes how others relate to us, but it also means that we have to make changes to how we look after ourselves. Our bodies are becoming capable of making babies, which means that we have to think carefully about sexual contact with others. Puberty also causes other changes, such as hair growth and increased smells in our sweat, which means that we will have to be more careful about staying clean.

# Young women

Girls' bodies are more obviously changed by puberty than boys' bodies. This is because women's bodies have to do much more of the work of sexual reproduction—making babies. Women's bodies will be able to create eggs, carry a fetus, give birth, and provide the baby with milk. Men's bodies only need to make and deliver sperm cells.

## Breasts

The first sign of puberty in girls is usually the development of breast buds behind the nipples. These will grow to make large glands, which can provide milk for a newborn baby. They are also an important part of becoming a woman, which can make us nervous or proud about their appearance. Left and right breasts can develop at different speeds—any differences will not be noticeable by the time they have finished growing. Exercises to "grow" breasts are a myth—but it is good to have well-toned muscles behind the breasts to help support them.

## It's your opinion

Girls choose to begin to wear a bra at different times—our mothers are probably best for advice on when to start. Wearing a bra early on is thought to help prevent sagging in later life. But some of us are embarrassed to wear a bra with a tiny cup size.

## Pubic and armpit hair

Puberty causes both boys and girls to begin to grow hair in new places. This hair is thicker and tougher than the soft "fluff" we had up until puberty. Pubic hair grows around the pubic bone and the vagina. Underarm hair also begins to grow.

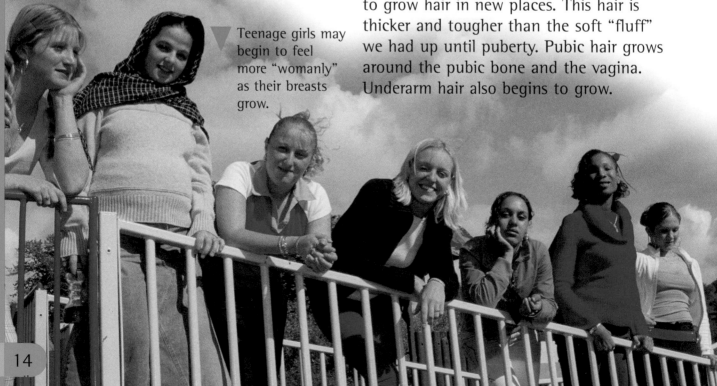

Teenage girls may begin to feel more "womanly" as their breasts grow.

Periods are driven by the monthly release of an egg by the ovary into the fallopian tube. ▶

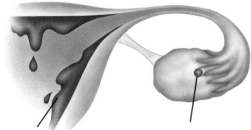

Lining of the uterus breaks down.

An egg develops inside one of the ovaries.

## Periods

The most dramatic change for girls is getting their period—the monthly shedding of the uterus lining, experienced as blood trickling from the vagina. The period is the result of a roughly four-week cycle in which the uterus lining builds up with blood and an egg matures in the ovary and travels down into the uterus. As long as it remains unfertilized, the egg will drop away along with the blood from the uterus's lining after about two weeks.

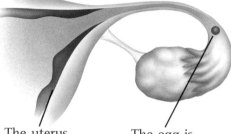

The uterus thickens.

The egg is released.

## When do they start?

Periods usually start around the age of 13 or 14, but many girls start them earlier or later. Each period lasts three to five days, although it is not unusual to have longer or shorter ones. It can take a while before periods become regular.

## Does it hurt?

Having a period can hurt a lot, a little, or not at all. A "cramping" feeling in the stomach can be eased by applying warmth or taking a mild painkiller. For most of us, the discomfort is less of an issue than feeling confident about managing our periods.

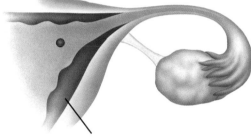

The uterus thickens more as the egg enters the uterus. If the egg is not fertilized, it passes out of the vagina with the blood from the uterus lining.

◀ Tampons, used with or without an applicator, allow activities such as swimming. However, some of us are more comfortable using pads.

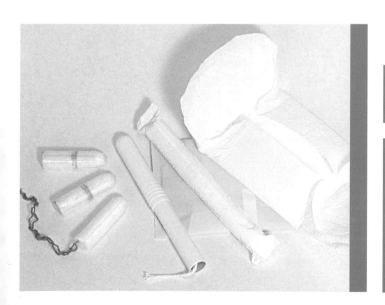

## It's your experience

"I felt awful. I couldn't even imagine how to go home because of the pain. I went to the school nurse and she gave me a couple of painkillers and a hot drink. I laid down with a hot water bottle, and I soon felt better and got back to class."

**Viki, age 15**

# Young men

Puberty makes definite changes to boys' bodies, but most of these changes are not clearly visible to others. Sexual maturity occurs as the testicles begin to produce sperm. The testicles "drop" clear of the body, inside the scrotal sac. Being at a distance from the body helps regulate their temperature—they need to be slightly cooler than average body temperature to produce sperm properly. The penis also grows.

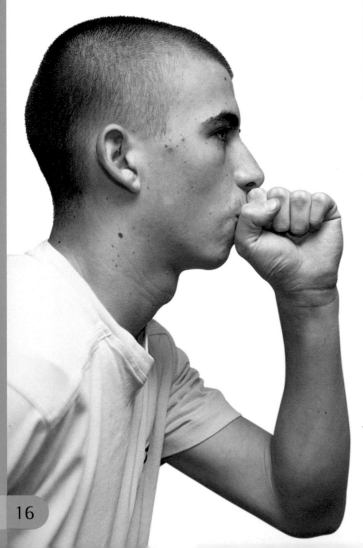

## It's your experience

"No one told me about wet dreams* until I had one. I didn't know what had happened in the morning, and felt too ashamed to tell my mom about the wetness on the bed sheets. Then I found out most boys have them, and it wasn't too bad—not like wetting the bed or something."

Spiro, age 14

* when boys ejaculate semen while sleeping

## Croak and squeak

Many boys find that the growth of the voice box, or larynx, from child-sized to adult-sized during puberty causes them to lose control of their voice. Sometimes, croaks or squawks accidentally slip out when we are speaking. Boys' voices undergo bigger changes than girls' voices, dropping by about an octave. One of the few external signs of male sexual maturity is the pronounced "bump" of cartilage in front of this enlarged voice box, known as the "Adam's apple."

As the voice box changes shape, boys' voices may croak or squeak. A quick cough can help regain control over the voice box.

Some boys are eager to grow facial hair as a sign of manliness. Others do not want it and prefer to shave from the first moment it appears.

## It's your decision

Some boys worry about penis size, especially if they start growing later than others. Other boys who started growing earlier may even tease them about how unmanly they are. Before getting upset, it is worth remembering that no one has a grown-up man's body before they are 18 or 19, so there's no point being worried or ashamed.

## Hair

Pubic hair appears on boys' bodies around the penis. Body hair grows under arms and on the chest, legs, arms, and lower half of the face. It does not all happen at the same time—and some boys will be more hairy than others, even when they are fully grown.

## Body shape

There are changes to boys' bodies that are less dramatic. As with girls, boys' faces become more "pointy," as the skull beneath changes shape and creates adult features. Boys' chests may also bulge at this time—instead of breasts, these bulges are the beginnings of pectoral muscles. Legs and feet often grow at different speeds than arms, so feeling gangly and clumsy is not unusual.

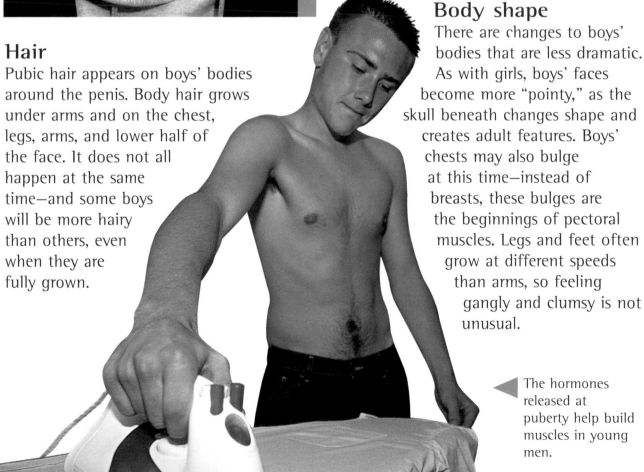

The hormones released at puberty help build muscles in young men.

# Hormones

How do our body parts know to start making all of these changes? They are triggered by a signal—a chemical message is sent out to the whole body via the bloodstream. Chemicals that have this signaling function are called hormones. Before puberty, a gland in the brain releases a hormone that "switches on" our gonads—a girl's ovaries or a boy's testicles. These "switched on" sex organs begin to produce the sex hormones that determine how our bodies develop; in girls, the main hormone is estrogen, and in boys, it is testosterone.

Boys and girls both need to wash their clothes more often to keep new smells under control.

## Hormone effects

Apart from the changes we have already seen, hormones can affect a range of other aspects of our bodies. Testosterone, for example, belongs to a group of body chemicals known as steroids. Like artificial steroids, testosterone can aid the formation of muscle tissue.

Hormones also trigger the release of special smells from our sweat glands. These smells would once have been important for making us attractive to potential mates but are likely to make us less attractive these days—so it's important to keep clean!

## It's your decision

As teenagers, most of us find that hormones during puberty seem to have a direct effect on our mood, causing us to be excited or sad. This is especially common for girls, whose hormone levels change throughout their monthly cycle. Keeping track of when your period is due will help you understand why you might be feeling down and reassure you that you'll feel differently in a few days.

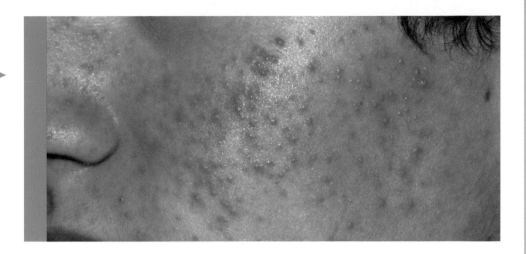

Acne is caused by sex hormones that upset the normal function of oil-producing glands in the skin.

## Pimples and acne

Skin needs to be oily to stay flexible and healthy, so our skin contains millions of tiny oil glands. For many of us, the arrival of hormones in our bloodstream will upset the oil glands, causing them to be blocked. A blocked gland is an easy place for bacteria to grow, and infections are soon visible as pimples. Regular pimples can be helped by washing with a bacteria-killing soap. But serious acne has nothing to do with hygiene, and it can only be treated by a doctor.

Hormones can change how your body feels, affecting your mood.

## It's your experience

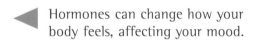

"I only found out about my mom's cycle when I started my periods. I hadn't noticed that she had days each month when she felt bad or grumpy. Then we started having them around the same days each month—it was like war. My dad had to leave the house sometimes!"

Mercedes, age 19

# Emotions

Although all of this change happens slowly, it can be confusing. We may feel more worried about what others think of us and less sure of ourselves. We may feel angry that other people have such power to influence our feelings or feel pleased when someone flatters us. These are normal emotional swings that most people experience as they settle into a more adult role.

Even the best students may find it hard to stay alert when they are feeling tired.

## Tiredness

For the reasons we have already looked at, this stage in our lives is often tiring. Tiredness typically makes us feel grumpy and irritable until we have had a nap. Being very tired can cause such emotional upset that we even have trouble getting to sleep! It's important not to confuse these feelings with being depressed—they are normal parts of growing up. Be kind to yourself, and let your body catch up on sleep on the weekends.

## It's your decision

It can be all too easy to lose our tempers when we are tired. If something is upsetting us or we are feeling irritable, it is worth pausing to decide what is happening. Is this problem really worth getting angry about, or would we feel better after a quick nap or some time to ourselves?

## Frustrations

Some of us will find this stage of our lives frustrating because we might think we should be allowed more freedom than a parent or a teacher gives us. It can be hard to find ways to show adults that we are responsible and deserving of more "space." At the same time, some of us find it difficult to be separated from parents—having to take care of ourselves can be frightening.

Strong emotions, such as anger, can upset us but are part of learning to cope with adult feelings.

## Sexual feelings

We can be surprised by how strong our feelings are toward people we find attractive. Sexual feelings can make us blush or have a hard time talking to someone we like. It can be embarrassing when other people realize what we're thinking, but it isn't the end of the world—and sometimes it is great to let other people know how we feel about them.

## It's your experience

"Every time I had to talk to her or be near her, I couldn't stop blushing. It didn't take long for people to notice and start making fun of it, but she didn't mind. We even went out together over the summer vacation."

Per, age 15

# Hygiene

The more grown-up we become, the more we are expected to take care of ourselves. This is especially true of keeping ourselves clean. Puberty gives our bodies new smells, and as we saw with hormones, it can also cause more pimples. So we do not just need to take over tasks our parents once helped us with—we also need to be more thorough than before.

## Washing

New smells mean that we need to wash thoroughly. Armpits, genitals, and feet are the most important places to soap and rinse every day.

During puberty, we sometimes notice that we develop odors around our genitals. If we wash every day, no one else will smell anything. We are more sensitive to our own body odors than other people are.

Fresh sweat usually will not smell too bad, but bacteria soon go to work on it, making it reek. Glands in the armpits make the strongest smells. ▼

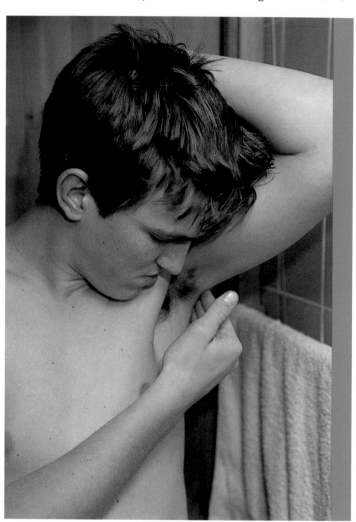

### It's your experience

"It's weird really smelling your own sweat for the first time. I didn't mind the smell too much, but I worried about other people smelling me."

Mona, age 18

## Take care

Use only gentle soaps on sensitive skin. Some of us will also want to wash our faces with soap, but this can dry out the skin. Skin needs natural oils, and soap takes this oil away. It is best to use a facial soap or a gentle cream designed to kill the bacteria that cause pimples. Many people start using deodorant.

## Body maintenance

We need to learn how to take care of ourselves, since we will eventually leave home as young adults. For example, many people leave home without learning to cut their toenails properly—straight across. Cutting nails badly can lead to ingrown toenails later in life, which can be painful and may require surgery. We also need to take care of our teeth and our hair and make regular dental and hair appointments.

## Hair removal

Boys may want to start shaving their faces. Girls often begin to remove the hair on their legs and underarms. As long as we keep clean and change our clothes, however, body hair is not a problem—it's a personal preference whether to remove it or not.

For legs and underarms, girls can try wax or hair-dissolving creams. If using blades to shave, soap or gel is needed to soften the hairs. It's important to use a clean razor and not to share razors with anyone else. Electric shavers are used on dry, unsoaped skin.

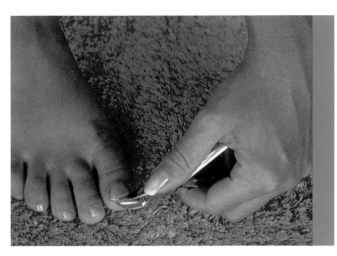

Learning to cut your toenails properly can prevent the risk of ingrown toenails later in life.

Some girls will grow unwanted facial hair. There are special creams for dissolving facial hair, which will not harm delicate skin. Creams are better than shaving, because regrowing hairs will have fine, soft ends, instead of scratchy "stubble."

## Hairstyles

Many of us experiment with our hair at this stage in our teens, finding new hairstyles or trying out ways to control our body hair.

## It's your decision

Shaving, waxing, and using hair-dissolving (depilatory) creams can be boring jobs but make some of us feel more attractive and confident. Before you decide if or how to control hair growth, bear in mind that it is a myth that shaved hair grows back thicker. If your hair is thickening up, that's just part of your normal development, not due to any hair removal method.

Is depilatory cream right for you?

# Exercise

During an average of two years of puberty, we usually grow about nine inches (23 cm). Organs such as our lungs grow even faster than the rest of our body to give us more strength and energy than we had before. This is the most important time in our lives to exercise. Training our bodies in these years can improve our health and fitness for the rest of our lives.

## Energy

Training our bodies with a hard physical challenge every day makes us more energetic. We can do anything that causes us to sweat from physical effort—a sports activity or a quick sprint on a bicycle, for example. Exercise is especially useful to help overcome the tiredness we may have in our teenage years—physical effort helps us sleep more deeply and wake up feeling more refreshed.

## It's your opinion

Which do you prefer, team sports or individual ones? Team sports can be good for learning how to work together with our friends and strategize against our opponents. Individual sports let us push ourselves to the limit and see what we are made of. Is one better than the other? Why?

## Control

As toddlers, it takes us a while to learn how to use our body smoothly and confidently. Sports help us develop this control during puberty as our bodies change shape and size, making it easier to be well-balanced and coordinated.

Sports help us learn how to control the whole range of movements our bodies can make.

Learning tricks on a bicycle might seem like fun, but this boy will be fitter and more coordinated as a result of having fun this way.

## It's your experience

"I think it's sad when people don't do enough activities to stay fit. I love that feeling of exhilaration after I've really pushed my body to its limit. I take every opportunity to use my body, even down to always walking up stairs rather than taking the elevator."

Nikko, age 18

## Types of activities

It is not necessary to be a sports fanatic to stay fit and well-exercised. Walking fast or biking to school, playing all kinds of games with friends, climbing trees, swimming, surfing, horseback riding, skateboarding, and dancing—each of these activities gives our bodies valuable exercise. It is good to do a variety of activities, since they each work our bodies in a different way.

## Menstrual pain

Having a period should not keep us from exercising. Gentle activity such as walking can actually help relieve menstrual pain. If you use tampons, you can even go swimming. A pad is enough for most other activities, although tampons may give us more confidence.

Swimming can be fun or a serious, competitive sport. Either way, it's one of the best workouts you can give your body, as well as a useful skill in emergencies!

# Diet

Diet affects many aspects of our health and may even be a factor in determining when puberty happens. Girls with poor nutrition or with very low body fat, for example, often begin their periods later than average. It is thought that improved nutrition in the developed world is a reason for the average age of puberty falling from about 15 to about 13 over the last 100 years.

## Don't worry

Unless we are very heavy or very light for our age, it is best not to worry too much about what we eat—as long as we are eating a range of different foods. Our bodies are growing, so they need more fuel than an adult body does. The best way to keep a healthy balance is to avoid snacking, keep exercising, and eat regular meals.

## It's your experience

"My friends like coming to my house because I've learned to cook from my mom and dad. I love seeing people enjoy my meals, and I find it really relaxing."

Tom, age 17

Most of us enjoy hamburgers, but high-fat foods are not all your body needs. Variety and balance are key to a good diet.

Fruits and vegetables, such as apples and carrots, are the best sources of vitamins and minerals, which we need to stay healthy.

## It's your decision

Should we eat a range of foods that are good for us or follow our instincts for a favorite treat? Some of us worry that our taste for treats creates pimples. Remember, fatty foods and sweets do not cause pimples—these are due to hormones that are not affected by our diet. But healthy foods with vitamin C (apples, oranges, tomatoes) and zinc (whole grain bread, nuts, seeds) can help keep our skin clear and healthy.

## Know your food groups

Our bodies need a range of nutrients to grow and maintain good health. It can be useful to know which of these nutrients can be found in which food items. If we know about the following types of nutrients, keeping a balanced diet is easy.

If you are not sure if your diet is balanced enough, check here to see if you are missing out on any nutrients.

| Nutrient | Function | Where we find them |
| --- | --- | --- |
| Protein | For body cells and growth | Milk, meat, fish, beans, nuts, cheese |
| Carbohydrate | Fuel | Cereals, bread, sugars, potatoes, rice, pasta |
| Fat | High-energy fuel, insulation | Oils, butter, cheese, fatty foods, meat |
| Fiber | Keeps bowels healthy | Any plant materials—cereals, fruit, and vegetables |
| Vitamins | Extra materials for health | Eggs, milk, fruit, vegetables, sunlight! |
| Minerals | Materials essential for bones and good body function | Milk, spinach, seafood, nuts, whole grains, fish |
| Water | Replaces lost water | Almost all food contains water—also try the sink! |

# Acting "grown up"?

Growing up lets us try more adult social roles than we have been able to before. We find ourselves and our friends becoming more interested in doing things we were not allowed to do (or couldn't cope with) as children. Partly, we just want to know what they are all about—but we also want to "prove" that we can handle them now.

▼ Becoming old enough to drive a vehicle is a major "rite of passage" for many boys and girls.

## Working

One good way to begin to explore adult roles is to take a simple part-time job—delivering newspapers or helping in a store, for example. In addition to learning about work and having adults relate to us more equally, we can also earn our own money and spend it more or less how we choose.

## Style

Around this time, we begin to find the style of person we want to be as adults. The urge to explore and express our adult role can make us put more effort into music or fashion. This might involve learning from adults we identify with, such as musicians, and adopting their style. For some of us, it may mean discovering more about a role that we would like to fill as adults—learning about art, science, or medicine, for example.

## Drink

There are laws that prevent children from buying alcoholic drinks and cigarettes. The age limit varies according to where we live in the world. Most teenagers see adults relaxing with a drink and enjoying themselves and want to try it as well. We need to remember that adults know from experience how much is enough. Most alcohol overdoses happen to children who drink too fast to realize how much they are being affected.

Young teens are perfect new customers for cigarette makers—most care more about being "grown up" than about dying early.

## Smoking

Some people think smoking is cool, and our friends can put a lot of pressure on us to join them in having a cigarette. It is worth remembering that smoking is extremely addictive and that many adults spend a great part of their lives trying to quit smoking. At any time, about 6 out of 10 smokers want to quit.

## Drugs

Some of us become interested in trying illegal drugs or other chemicals, such as glue, that can make us "high." We might try a drug on a dare or because we think it will make us happy. We need to remember that, like alcohol, most drugs pose a risk to our health and that buying or using most of them can give us a criminal record. It is not weak to refuse a dare to take drugs. If you think there is any chance you might take a drug, look for reliable drug safety information.

### It's your experience

"My older brother smoked, and my best friend used to sneak out with him when he was at our place. So I ended up going along with them and trying it out. It made me feel sick at first, but then I got used to it."

Ben, age 14

### It's your opinion

Do you think there are good reasons to take drugs? How important do you think it is that some drugs are illegal? Is it better to use legal stimulants such as alcohol? Is safety or legality more important? What would you do if someone close to you changed his or her behavior because of drugs?

# Sex

Since sexual maturity is the main result of puberty, it is hardly surprising that the adult activity most of us become curious about is sex. As we reach our mid-teens, some of us may worry that our friends have all "done it" and that they think we are backward. There are good reasons to wait to have sex. Also, research has shown that a lot more teenagers claim to have sexual experience than actually do.

Sexual intimacy is important for adults to express love and to feel loved. For most of us, just being close is a good start.

## What sex is

Some of us treat all sorts of pleasurable contact with another person as sex. The technical definition of sex, however, includes intercourse—when a man places his penis inside a woman's vagina. Sperm cells enter the woman from the man's penis. At the fertile time of a woman's cycle, the sperm will be able to fertilize her egg, making her pregnant. Adults have sex to express their love for each other, for pleasure, and to make babies.

## Sex secrets?

Sex is the most private and intimate experience most of us will have as grown-ups. It usually involves us in a relationship of trust and respect with the other person, which means that most of us dislike talking about our sex lives in public. If you are talking about your experience with a friend, think about how comfortable you would be if your sexual partner was doing the same.

This normal desire for secrecy can make it hard for parents and their sexually-active teens to communicate. Instead of talking about our experiences, it can help to discuss sex in theory—reassuring our parents that we know about safe sex, for example.

### It's your experience

"It's like, you have a guy that you supposedly fall in love with—and I say 'supposedly' because you're kind of young to really know what love is—and you'll do anything to stay with him. A lot of girls are like that."

Sara, age 15 (pregnant)

### It's your decision

Some of us believe you should never have sex without thinking carefully—for example, about the person, the situation, and issues such as birth control or sexually transmitted diseases. Others feel we shouldn't worry about taking a risk now and then. Where do you strike the balance?

Parents and teens need to figure out ways to cope with their changing status and relationship with each other.

## Your call

Having sex for the first time can be a daunting experience. Once we are old enough, it is our decision, alone, when the time is right for us. For some of us, it will be when we meet a person we like or love. For others, it will be after we are married.

## Know the law

In most countries, sex is illegal for people younger than 16. The law also reminds us that we are not adults yet, no matter how grown-up we may feel. We are still not fully aware of all the issues, risks, and responsibilities involved in adult relationships. But the law is not normally used to punish us if we admit that we have had sex or if we need help for any reason.

# Sexual health

If we choose to have sex outside of marriage, it is likely that we will have more than one sexual partner over time. There are two consequences to think about: an unwanted pregnancy and the risk of contracting a sexually transmitted disease.

## Diseases

Some germs spread by sexual contact. They are called STDs, or sexually transmitted diseases. STDs can be harmless, or they can cause health problems such as liver disease or even death. HIV, the virus that causes AIDS, is an STD.

About 1 in every 100 young adults in the richest 10 countries of the world are carriers of chlamydia, which can cause women to become infertile. The best way to avoid these infections is to avoid all sexual contact. The next best way is to use a condom.

### It's your experience

"I was so relieved when the test came back negative. When John told me he had herpes, I was so angry that he hadn't told me before we had sex. I can't bear the idea of having herpes for the rest of my life, even if it doesn't kill you or anything."

**Pip, age 17**

 Levels of STD infections are closely related to poverty. Poor people's lack of healthcare makes them more vulnerable to STDs.

## Estimated occurrence and annual incidence of curable STDs* by region

| Region | Population aged 15-49 years (million) | Occurrence per 1,000 of population | Annual Incidence (million) |
|---|---|---|---|
| North America | 156 | 19 | 14 |
| Western Europe | 203 | 20 | 17 |
| North Africa & Middle East | 165 | 21 | 10 |
| Eastern Europe & Central Europe | 205 | 29 | 22 |
| Sub-Saharan Africa | 269 | 119 | 69 |
| South & Southeast Asia | 955 | 50 | 151 |
| East Asia & Pacific | 815 | 7 | 18 |
| Australia & New Zealand | 11 | 27 | 1 |
| Latin America & Caribbean | 260 | 71 | 38 |
| Total | 3,040 | (average = 40) | 340 |

* Herpes, gonorrhea, chlamydia

# Pregnancy

Many of us have heard untrue stories about how to avoid becoming pregnant. Having sex standing up or trying to stop intercourse before the man releases sperm are both useless methods. It is also not true that young women are safe from pregnancy the first few times they have sex. Although there are more days in the month when a woman is not fertile than fertile, it takes great skill to figure out when they are.

There are only two reliable approaches to preventing pregnancy: avoiding sex altogether or using birth control methods such as condoms or doctor-prescribed pills.

## It's your experience

"I always wore a condom, but I was only putting it on for the last few minutes. We didn't know that some sperm get out way before then. So when she said she had missed her period, I didn't believe her. It was bad, really scary."

**No name given, age 17**

▲ If you are at the right stage in your life, learning the due date for your unborn baby is a happy event.

## Health support

If we have any problems or questions about our sexual health, our doctor or local family planning clinic can usually provide us with support and advice. If we have unprotected sex or have an accident with a burst condom, for example, it is a good idea to visit a doctor immediately for a health check and advice.

◄ Health advisers are understanding and helpful.

# Self-image

All of us feel awkward or embarrassed at some point in our lives—but we shouldn't be ashamed of these feelings. These feelings help us try harder and do better in the future. They can help us improve the skills we will need for our adult lives. Without these feelings, we would not be able to adapt properly to sharing our lives with other people. We should never feel ashamed because of what we look like or where we come from. What we are trying to be is far more important.

Our bodies give unconscious signals when we feel awkward.

## Clumsiness

There are good reasons for feeling a bit awkward in our growing bodies. They are always changing and can seem oddly-shaped during these years. We are also a lot more aware of what we are doing and how we look to other people than we were as children. It can be hard even to walk properly when we suddenly think about what we are doing. These feelings pass as we grow older. Taking up a sport (see page 24) can also help.

### It's your experience

"I tipped my plate upside down when I was telling a story to an older boy I really liked. My food went flip, right under the plate, and everyone looked at us. I felt really embarrassed."

Ruth, age 16

When we are relaxed with friends, we forget to be embarrassed. ▶

## Sexual role

It is normal to be unsure about how well we are "playing the role" of being a young man or a young woman; we are new to it, after all. For most of us, it matters enough that we tend to worry if someone criticizes or teases us—telling a boy he is like a girl, for example. The more experience we get, the more confident we become about how well we are doing, so we don't worry about teasing as much.

## You've got it

It is good for all of us to find the features of our appearance that we like. The parts of our appearance that we can change, such as how we wear our hair or which clothes we like, become our trademark. It is up to us: do we want to have fun with our clothes, keep up with the latest or most expensive fashions, be sporty, or let people know that we are not interested in all of that? Appearances are a kind of role-play that we have a lot of control over.

◀ Choosing how to look can be a big responsibility.

## Mirror, mirror

It's normal to spend some time during our early teens wondering how we look or to take some time to try out a few expressions in the mirror. Most of us will experience teasing because we look different in one way or another. In the end, how people see us will always depend more on how we behave than on how we look, so we should never take appearances too seriously.

## It's your opinion

▶ More young people are heavily-built than ever before. Some argue that obesity is dangerous for health and looks ugly. Others say that no one has the right to say what size someone else should be or argue that big is beautiful. What do you think? Are there good reasons to think that slim is sexy?

# Under pressure

There can be many challenges at this time in our lives. We try to figure out how to become young adults. We have to find new ways to relate to our family. We try out new friendships and new feelings. At the same time, we learn a lot about the wider world at school—and go through tests and exams. It can be a lot to cope with, especially when all of the physical growth makes us tired half of the day. It is not surprising that we sometimes feel a bit stressed.

## Peer pressure

Of all the pressures we have to cope with and learn from, the demands and expectations of our friends are usually the most important to us. Friends and other "peers"—people we know who are about the same age as us—can sometimes do or say things that upset us or lead us to make mistakes. But by sharing what they know and encouraging each other, friends can also help each other grow and conquer new experiences.

It can be challenging being friends with someone who has expensive things—we always want to catch up.

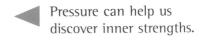

Pressure can help us discover inner strengths.

## School stress

Exams can be scary, especially if the results will decide where we go next in the education system. Part of the purpose of exams is to teach us how to cope with being "put to the test," helping us to learn how to deal with stress. Sometimes, the challenge of an exam drives us to learn better and remember more; at other times, we may have to accept that we did not do as well as we had hoped. Both experiences can be good practice for the challenges of adult life.

## Good pressure

Some pressure is a good thing for most of us—with nothing pushing us, most of us would probably waste a lot of time doing things that are not interesting or satisfying, such as watching a lot of TV. When people make demands on us, we have to learn to do new things and acquire new talents. So in some ways, we are lucky if we have people around us who will challenge us to grow and learn.

Exams challenge us not only to learn, but also to deal with stress.

## It's your decision

As we grow up, we gain more freedom to decide which pressures we are happy to accept. For example, we can decide whether or not to take part in organized activities beyond school. Some of us will use this freedom to get away from pressures; others prefer to get involved. Which option suits you?

# Relationships

In our mid- to late-teens, most of us know what it is like to feel passionately attracted to someone. Our bodies are now fully equipped for our adult roles as men and women, and some of our emotions have changed, too. Having a grown-up relationship can be hard, though. We are still not completely independent, so we need to negotiate how much freedom we deserve with our parents. Also, we are still learning and changing rapidly, so our relationships suffer if they cannot cope with those changes.

Crushes can be awkward and embarrassing, but they can also be important. They let us explore our feelings before we have to cope with a relationship.

## Crushes and love

From early puberty, and perhaps before, some of us experience strong obsessions with other people. These crushes are usually one-way, secret things. They are a kind of rehearsal, letting us get a feel for what it might be like to be in a two-way, loving relationship. Proper relationships are more complicated and are more likely to cause us distress as well as happiness.

## It's your opinion

Our first serious loving relationship often feels like it is the first time anyone ever really loved anyone. We can't believe our parents or anyone else ever had such a strong passion and refuse to believe that it could ever be broken. Adults tend to expect these loves not to last because they remember how it was for them. Who's right? Do you think teenage romances can last forever?

## Best buddies

For many of us, the strongest relationships we have throughout puberty will not be sexual. We may have one or a few close friends who understand us very well and with whom we like to spend as much free time as possible. These friendships are just as important as sexual relationships in teaching us how to be a good companion in adult life. Sometimes, they can be tricky to maintain into adulthood.

## Keeping and sharing

A lot of what we think and feel at this time is personal and very hard to share—some of it is best kept secret or filed away in a personal diary. But it is also important to share many of our thoughts with the people we love and trust. A fresh point of view on something that is troubling us can sometimes make all the difference.

▲ Sending a valentine's card can be a way for some people to express their feelings, either secretly or openly.

## It's your experience

"I've never felt like this before. When I'm with her, nothing else matters. Even shadows on the street will remind me of times when we were together. I just want to be with her all the time."

Ben, age 15

# Dealing with adults

As we stop being children and become young adults, our relationships with our parents and other adults change. We can look after ourselves better, but we have to prove to adults that they can relax and trust us to be sensible. This can be a slow and frustrating process for us as growing teenagers. Sometimes, it can seem as if our parents will never recognize the grown-up side of us, but we have to remember that they know us better than anyone else.

## It's your decision

Imagine you had a pet animal that lived in the pocket of your coat, demanded hugs, and needed grooming and feeding every hour for 12 years—then it jumped out and disappeared, only turning up briefly for meals. Before we get upset at our parents, can we imagine how strange this is for them?

## Letting go

There can be other difficulties for our parents as we grow older. We are less likely to need them or turn to them for comfort and advice as we become more independent. They can feel like they are being left out of our life and may find it hard to let go after so many years of focusing on caring for us.

▼ Teen years can be the hardest for a parent and child's relationship. At times, both sides may feel misunderstood or trapped.

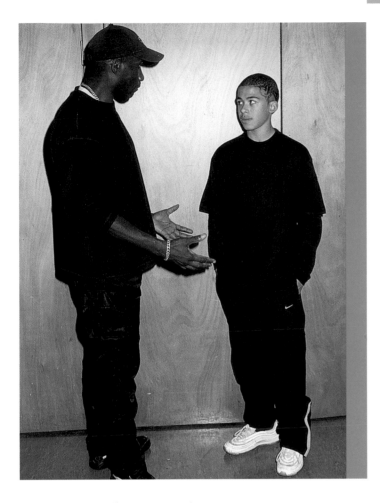

## Sexual maturity

As we grow to fill our roles as young men or women, our sexual maturity becomes more obvious to the adults we meet. Some adults may find this embarrassing and hard to ignore, and others may assume that we are completely grown up and interested in sexual relationships. As with everything else we encounter as we grow up, we each need to learn to recognize and understand these new experiences and find ways to deal with them. However, if an adult makes you uneasy or tries to meet with you in secret, tell a parent about it.

Professional advisers are there to help us cope with new experiences. It is usually much scarier thinking about talking to someone than actually being there.

## It's your decision

Some of us believe that our experiences are there for us to figure out for ourselves; running to an adult for help can seem childish. But sometimes adults have great advice or know a simple solution to something we cannot figure out. Is it better to call for help or to figure things out alone?

Some adults have experience helping young adults with the more routine challenges we face. It's up to us to find an adult whose advice we can respect.

## Independent advice

Usually, we can rely on our family and friends for advice and suggestions, but sometimes we would prefer independent advice. Most schools and health services provide ways to get advice when you need it. Conversations you have with counselors or medical staff are normally confidential (kept private), but it may be worth checking first.

# Glossary

**Acne** a malfunction of oil glands in the skin, creating a rash of pimples or "zits"

**Celibacy** not having sexual relationships

**Coming-of-age** becoming sexually mature, capable of reproduction

**Commitment** promises to each other

**Conception** when a fertilized ovum (egg) implants in the lining of the uterus (womb)

**Condom** Form of contraception that places a barrier between sperm and egg

**Consent** agree

**Contraception** prevention of pregnancy

**Depilatory** a cream that dissolves hairs

**Estrogen** a female sex hormone that prepares the woman for ovulation (the release of an ovum from a fallopian tube); estrogen is used in the contraceptive pill

**Fertilization** when a sperm and ovum (egg) join together to create the beginnings of a new life

**Genitals** sexual organs, such as a vagina or penis

**Gland** a body part with a specific function, usually producing a substance

**Heterosexual** person who is sexually attracted to the opposite sex

**Hormone** chemicals produced by special glands in the body that carry messages to particular organs or tissues

**Identify** feel a connection with, a shared attitude or style

**Infertile** unable to conceive children

**Intimacy** a feeling of closeness that is personal and private

**Limbs** extensions from the central body, i.e., arms and legs

**Maturity** physical or emotional quality of being fully-formed

**Nutrient** a substance required by an organism for its survival

**Pectoral** flat muscle beneath the nipple on both the male and the female chest

**Period** shedding of the lining of the uterus, roughly every 28 days if fertilization has not occurred; also called menstruation

**Procreation** producing children

**Puberty** the period in a person's life when his or her body is sexually maturing

**Pubic hair** hair appearing during puberty, especially on and around the pubis (above the genitals)

**Reproduction** producing children

**Sex cells** the egg, or ovum (female), or sperm (male) cell

**Sexually transmitted disease (STD)** any disease that is passed on through sexual contact, for example HIV/AIDS or genital herpes

**Sweat** salty liquid emitted by the skin to help lower body temperature

**Testosterone** male sex hormone promoting muscle growth and other male attributes

# Further information

**Puberty 101**

Answers your questions about puberty, sexually transmitted diseases, drugs, and mental health.

www.puberty101.com

**Teen Puberty**

Provides answers to your questions about male and female puberty, general and psychological health, and more.

www.teenpuberty.com

**I Wanna Know**

A beginner's guide to puberty with information on physical and emotional changes, as well as tips for surviving puberty.

www.iwannaknow.org/puberty

**Cool Nurse**

General information on puberty, as well as fitness and nutrition information and other tips.

www.coolnurse.com/puberty.htm

**Teen Advice**

Provides links to several Internet resources to help you deal with all of the changes that puberty brings.

www.teenadvice.about.com/od/puberty

**Stand Up Girl**

A site for teenage mothers and mothers-to-be. It has an antiabortion agenda.

www.standupgirl.com

**Note to parents and teachers:** Because of the nature of the subject matter and the Internet, these Web sites may contain material that is inappropriate for some young people. We therefore strongly advise that Internet access be supervised by a responsible adult.

# Index